Alphabet Monsters

by
Amy Gray

For my little Elowyn

The **A** monster is an
alien

He's a slimy, gooey alien
Who lives among the stars
His favourite food is moon cake
And his favourite planet is Mars

Aa

Can you name the alien?

The B monster is a
bad bee

She's busy being a bad little bee
Bursting balloons and bubbles
Better not touch her beehive
Or you'll be in big, big trouble

What sound does she make?

The C monster is a
colourful crab

Clickety clickety CLICK CLICK CLICK
Red, blue, orange, and yellow
The colourful crab is bold and bright
But he's a very snippy fellow!

Can you click like a crab?

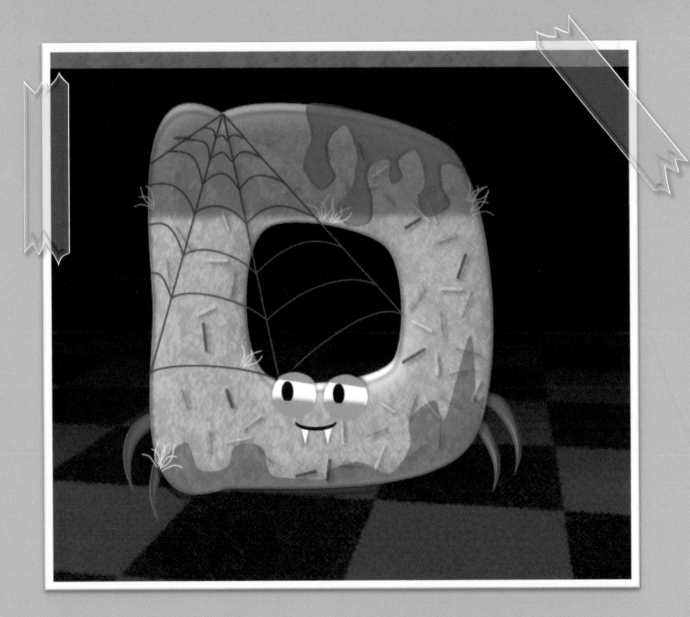

The D monster is a
dirty doughnut

Lurking beneath the dark, damp fridge
Hiding out of sight
For if she dares to venture out
Somebody might take a bite

Dd

Would you eat a dirty doughnut?

The E monster has
eight eyes

It sees you here, it sees you there
And everywhere you go
But never look it in the eyes
It's rude to stare, you know!

Ee

Can you count its eyes?

The F monster is a
funny flower

You'll find her in the forest
Laughing with the mice
She loves to frighten foxes
Because she isn't very nice!

What colour is the flower?

The **G** monster is made of
gingerbread

The giant gingerbread monster
Has buttons of green and grey
And if you try to eat them
You will frighten her away

What other words begin with G?

The H monster looks like a
hedgehog

Happy little H monster
Hiding in the grass
He tries to catch the grasshoppers
But he can't move very fast

Is he soft or spiky?

The I monster is an
ice-cream

The I monster lives in an igloo
To keep him out of trouble
If he starts to get too hot
He'll turn into a puddle

Is ice-cream cold or hot?

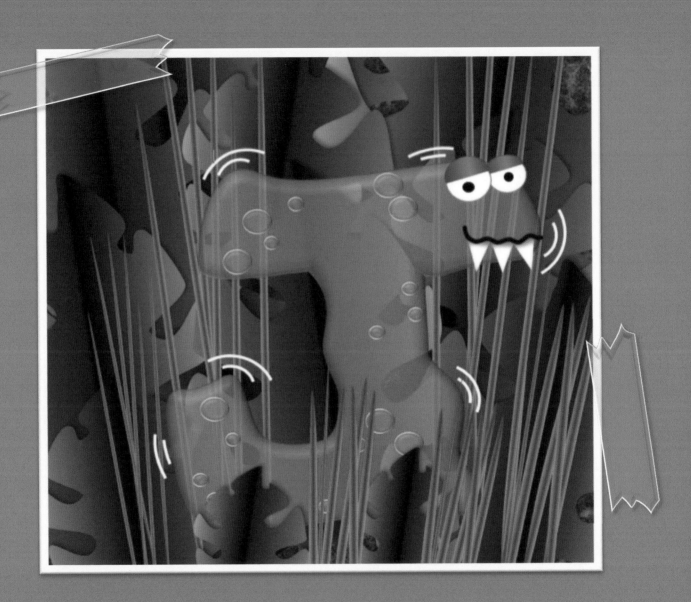

The J monster is a
jiggly jelly

Jiggling jelly j monster
Is a wibbly, wobbly bundle
He loves to jump and bounce around
And jiggle in the jungle

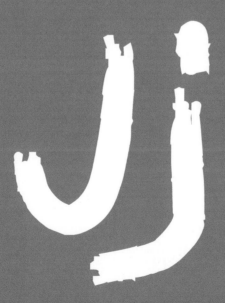

What colour is this monster?

The K monster is a
kind king

The K monster is a royal king
Who loves to fly a kite
He has large teeth just like a shark
But you know he'll never bite

What other words begin with K?

The L monster is a
loud ladybird

She roars loudly like a lion
I'm sure you will have heard
And although she's only little
She's a mighty ladybird

What is the opposite of loud?

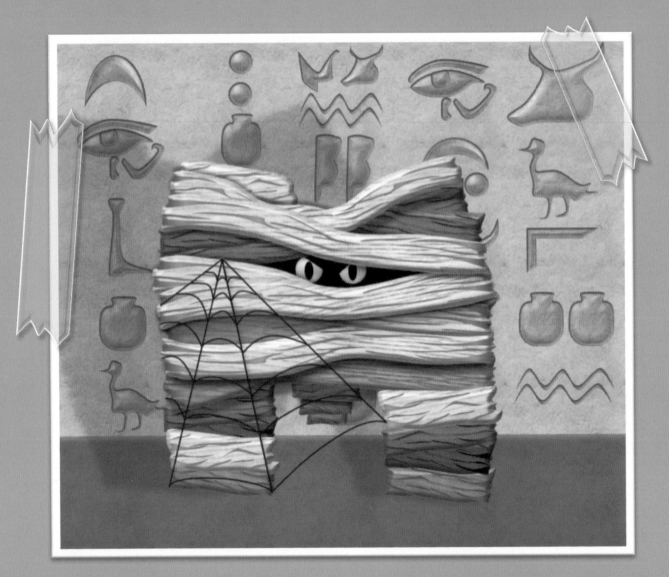

The **M** monster is a
mummy

Beneath an ancient pyramid
This monster may be found
You might not hear her mumbling
From a mile underground

Mm

Can you name the mummy?

The N monster is
NOISY

The noisy night–time monster
Will wake you from your dreams
He shouts, bangs and claps his hands
And shakes his tambourines

How many arms does he have?

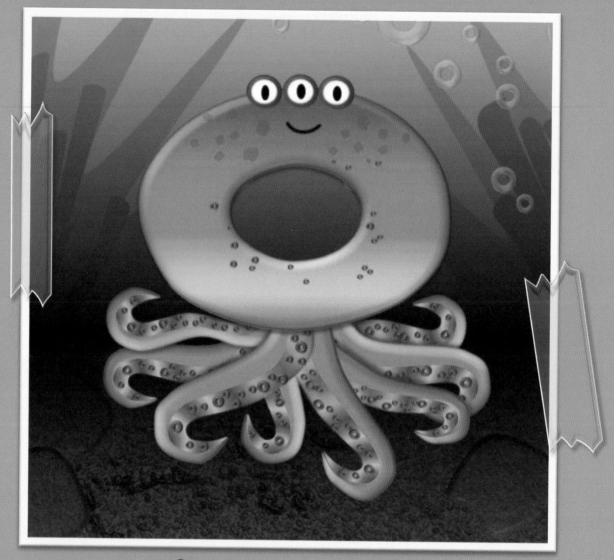

The O monster is an
orange octopus

The O monster is orange
Eight tentacles and three eyes
It loves to go to the coral reef
To eat all the cod pies

What animals live in the ocean?

The P monster is a
pizza

She's a sloppy slice of pizza
Hiding in a pizza box
And when you are not looking
She'll jump out and eat your socks

Pp

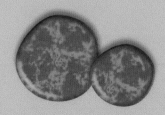

What foods start with P?

The Q monster is
QUICK

Upon his getaway skateboard
The quick Q monster rides
He steals pears and bananas
And quietly he hides

What is the opposite of quick?

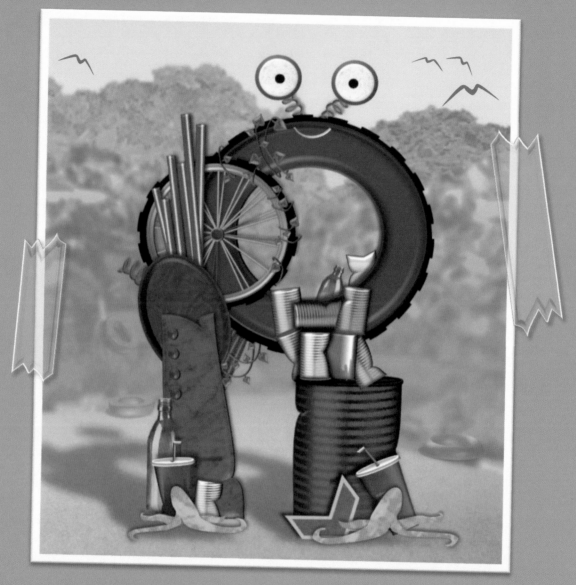

The R monster
recycles

It's the rattling, recycling monster
Seeking treasures of all kinds
Rusty, broken or dented
Reusing everything he finds

What does recycle mean?

The S monster is a
sandy snake

She's a sandy, snaky monster
Who loves the sea and sun
Slithering over seaweed
Is her idea of fun

Ss

What is the S monster wearing?

The T monster looks like a
tiger

He's stripy like a tiger
With ten teeth and ten claws
This monster is not a scary guy
He's just two inches tall

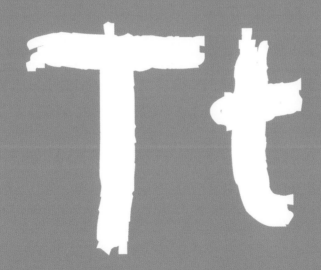

Can you count to 10?

The U monster is a
unicorn

It lurks deep in the forest
With its pointy, colourful horn
This graceful, unique creature
Is a rainbow unicorn

How many eyes does it have?

The **V** monster looks like a
vampire bat

Invisible in the darkness
Hovering above the trees
Searching for an evening snack
Of bugs and slugs and fleas

Can you name the V monster?

The W monster is a
watermelon

It's a wild watermelon
Green with pink inside
Now, melons are not scary
Until they're six feet wide

What other words begin with W?

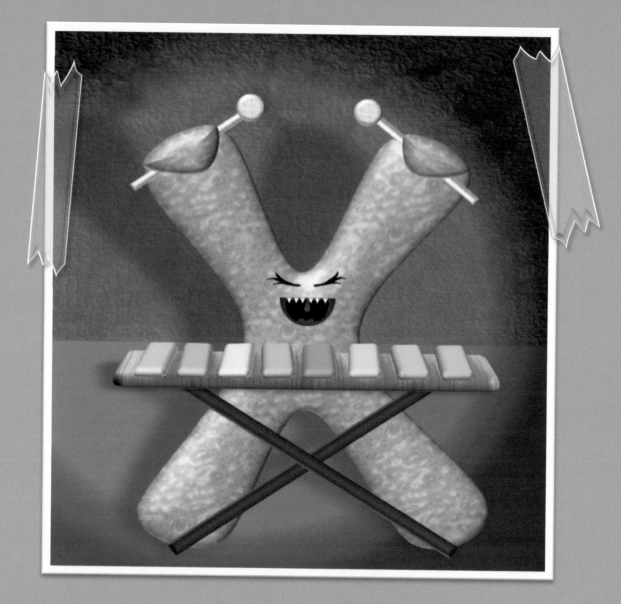

The X monster plays the
xylophone

It's the extraordinary x monster
With exciting colourful keys
Don't ask him to be quiet
Or he'll try to play your knees

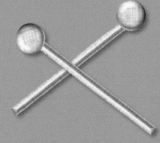

What colours are his keys?

The Y monster is
yellow

Yes, it's the yellow y monster
Sunny, sparkly and bright
At dawn she yawns so loudly
She'll wake you with a fright

Can you do a big yawn?

The **Z** monster is a
zig zag

The zig zag z loves jazz music
And drinks anything that's fizzy
She'll dazzle you with her crazy dance
And stops when she gets dizzy

Do your best crazy dance

Printed in Great Britain
by Amazon